W9-CEK-580

FARMERS

by Charly Haley

Cody Koala
An Imprint of Pop!
popbooksonline.com

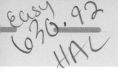
abdopublishing.com
Published by Pop!, a division of ABDO, PO Box 398166, Minneapolis, Minnesota 55439. Copyright © 2019 by POP, LLC. International copyrights reserved in all countries. No part of this book may be reproduced in any form without written permission from the publisher. Pop!™ is a trademark and logo of POP, LLC.

Printed in the United States of America, North Mankato, Minnesota

042018
092018
♺ **THIS BOOK CONTAINS RECYCLED MATERIALS**

Cover Photo: iStockphoto
Interior Photos: iStockphoto, 1, 13; Shutterstock Images, 5 (top), 5 (bottom left), 5 (bottom right), 6, 9 (top), 9 (bottom left), 9 (bottom right), 10, 15, 16, 17, 19 (top), 19 (bottom left), 19 (bottom right), 21

Editor: Meg Gaertner
Series Designer: Laura Mitchell

Library of Congress Control Number: 2017963076

Publisher's Cataloging-in-Publication Data

Names: Haley, Charly, author.
Title: Farmers / by Charly Haley.
Description: Minneapolis, Minnesota : Pop!, 2019. | Series: Community workers | Includes online resources and index.
Identifiers: ISBN 9781532160103 (lib.bdg.) | ISBN 9781532161223 (ebook) |
Subjects: LCSH: Farmers--Juvenile literature. | Agriculture--Juvenile literature. | Farmers--United States--Juvenile literature. | Occupations--Careers--Jobs--Juvenile literature. | Community life--Juvenile literature.
Classification: DDC 630.203--dc23

Hello! My name is

Cody Koala

Pop open this book and you'll find QR codes like this one, loaded with information, so you can learn even more!

Scan this code* and others like it while you read, or visit the website below to make this book pop.

popbooksonline.com/farmers

*Scanning QR codes requires a web-enabled smart device with a QR code reader app and a camera.

Table of Contents

Chapter 1

A Day in the Life

Farmers produce food.

Some farmers grow **crops**,

such as vegetables or grains.

Others raise animals for

meat, milk, or eggs.

Watch a video here!

Farmers wake up early and work many hours each day outside. They must watch the weather to make sure their crops and animals do not get hurt.

Chapter 2

The Work

Some farmers raise cows for milk. They hook the cows up to machines that milk them. The milk can be made into cheese or yogurt.

Complete an activity here!

Many farmers raise **livestock** for meat. These animals include cows, chickens, and pigs.

> Farm animals must be cared for and fed every single day.

Farmers also plant seeds in large fields. They plant corn, wheat, soybeans, and other crops. Farmers **harvest** their crops when they are ready to be eaten.

Chapter 3

Tools for Farmers

Farmers keep their animals and tools in barns. Farmers drive **tractors** that pull different machines through the fields.

Learn more here!

Farmers use a **plow** to
turn dirt in a field. This makes
it easier to plant seeds in
the ground.

Farmers use a **planter** to
plant many seeds in rows.

Farmers also use machines that help them harvest their crops quickly. A **combine** is used to harvest grain.

A combine cuts down crops and separates out the parts that can be eaten.

Chapter 4

Helping the Community

Farmers produce most of the food that people eat. The crops, meat, and milk that farmers sell go into grocery stores and markets. Farmers feed the community.

Learn more here!

Making Connections

Text-to-Self

If you had your own farm, what animals or crops would you like to have there?

Text-to-Text

Have you read other books about community workers? How are their jobs different from a farmer's?

Text-to-World

Farmers are important community workers. What do you think the world would be like without farmers?

Glossary

combine – a machine used to harvest grain.

crops – plants grown by farmers, usually for food.

harvest – to gather or pick crops.

livestock – animals raised by farmers.

planter – a machine used by farmers to plant seeds.

plow – a machine used by farmers to prepare land to plant crops.

tractor – a vehicle driven by farmers in fields.

Index

Online Resources

popbooksonline.com

Thanks for reading this Cody Koala book!

Scan this code* and others like it in this book, or visit the website below to make this book pop!

popbooksonline.com/farmers

*Scanning QR codes requires a web-enabled smart device with a QR code reader app and a camera.